Some Things are Worse than Being

Older than

Dirt

Ben Goode

Illustrated by
David Mecham

The Truth About Life ™

Published by:
Apricot Press
Box 1611
American Fork, Utah
84003

books@apricotpress.com
www.apricotpress.com

ISBN 1-885027-11-7

Cover Design & Layout by David Mecham
Printed in the United States of America

1st Edition published in 1999
2nd Edition published in 2000
Re-printed in 2002, 2003

"What is this decimating scourge?" You ask. Is it Aids, hate crimes, gout, or failure to post signs on restaurant doors warning that microwave ovens are in use? No, it is a disease that's right before your eyes only you just can't see it without your bifocals: It's OLD AGE and I'll wager hardly a family alive has not lost at least one precious loved one to this ruthless and debilitating scourge.

Contents

A message of hope

This book was written to give hope to millions. For instance, I, the author, am full of hope. I hope I don't die in my sleep. I hope I don't have to wake up 6 times tonight to go to the bathroom. I hope I can stay awake to see who won the ball game. I hope I can find my glasses. I hope I have a good bowel movement today. I hope I can find my way home. I hope they don't take away my driver's license. I hope this stuff they're feeding me is really food. I hope my social security check comes before someone else wins the lottery.

So, as you can see, hope is an important character trait to develop. The problem is, there are many older people wandering around without much hope. Being full of this high degree of hope myself, I decided that the most humane thing I could do for the rest of my life would be to share my bright outlook, this glimmer of hope, with my other aging readers. I sincerely hope you enjoy my efforts.

- Ben Goode

1 How to Find Peace and Happiness After the World has Symbolically Hurled You Aside onto the Trash Heap of Life

A few years ago, I wrote a book entitled Geezerhood: What to expect from life now that you're as old as dirt. I kind of figured that I would be dead long before I could ever get rich from the royalties. Well, here it is a few years later, and guess what: I'm not completely dead yet, and I'm still not rich. Besides, my fingers still work, and so I am capable of sitting around using my dementia to conjure up wild fantasies that have become all jumbled up with my real-life memories, which sometimes makes for entertaining reading. Also, I've found that my friends and associates, who are still alive, are not yet too tired or miserable to stop whining. They must be heard. Besides, I think I might like to make one final, feeble try at becoming a rich old geezer, and so I've written another book. Like the last one, this book tells it like it is and really gives you some shocking and revolutionary ground-breaking information to think about. Unfortunately, none of it is based on sound research or for that matter, even the truth, but it does have a pretty catchy title intended to sucker bored people into believing that it contains some useful information.

We're hoping, that at the very least, if you are at all concerned with growing older, this book will give you a little brighter outlook on life, that it just might soften the impact of the blow when you come to the knowledge that it really is true that now you're pretty much just taking up space. We're afraid that if the notion that old people are worthless gets wide circulation, it could cause senior citizens to become depressed. In order to head off wide-spread depression, we've written this chapter. If there's anything the older generation needs, it's perspective. Try this:

These are some things worse than being older than dirt:

1. Going to the hospital to have your appendix removed and having the doctors tie your intestines, bladder, and colon into tight granny knots as a practical joke.

2. Having the dog you're neutering get hold of the scalpel and turn on you.

3. Sky diving while chained to a walrus.

4. Running off to fight the Barbarians and realizing as you get into the heat of battle that, instead of your battle ax, you grabbed your rubber chicken.

5. Waking up next to another corpse.

6. After 5 kids and 25 years of marriage, finding out that your husband is really only a cartoon character.

7. Throwing a stick out into a river for your beloved pet retriever, Sparky, to chase and discovering too late that the river is filled with piranha.

8. Having your toilet explode while you're sitting on it.

9. Catching a quick nap and realizing that while you were sleeping, the construction guys have used your head to put behind the wheel of a huge, loaded dump truck to keep it from rolling backward down the hill.

10. Being trapped inside a cave for two months and having to survive by eating vegemite.

11. After a great day with the grandkids at the water park wondering why, on such a nice day, you have the place all to yourself, then finding out the reason when you get arrested by the police for trespassing in what turns out to be the city sewer treatment plant.

12. Needing a favor from a politician.

13. Having a bad coughing spell and watching helplessly as your last 6 remaining teeth fly out your mouth.

14. Having a bad coughing spell and watching helplessly as your heart's pacemaker flies out your mouth.

15. Having a bad coughing spell and watching helplessly as a hive of mad wasps flies out your mouth.

16. Having a bad coughing spell and watching helplessly as the stitches from your open-heart surgery go flying out your mouth.

17. Sneezing up an alien.

18. Being frozen in suspended animation for 2000 years and for the entire time being unable to get an annoying song out of your head.

19. Sticking your hand down a gopher hole and finding a wolverine.

20. In order to try and cure your cancer of the armpits, having the doctors place you on a strict diet of toads and rutabaga.

21. Listening to your neighbors' grandchild's band concert.

22. Having as your only way to keep from freezing to death, using your arm hairs as thread to stitch a new coat out of the rat skins you have harvested in your Siberian prison cell.

23. Hitting a bull moose while going 70 miles per hour on your Vespa motor scooter.

24. When you wind up in Hades, finding out that loud rap music is piped over all of the loud speakers.

25. Being arrested for jay-walking in the country of Saddamistan and having the judge sentence you to being beaten to death with zucchini.

26. Watching your doctor remove your age spots with a power sander.

27. Being eaten by gerbils.

28. On Thanksgiving Day, with the whole family there, realizing as you open the oven that during all the commotion, you chained the frozen turkey up outside and now, all you have to serve a house full of guests is your former mutt, Scooter, "medium well", and some pretty good stuffing.

29. Kissing a 6-foot, 200 pound frog and finding that it's only a frog.

30. Being accused in public of being a politician.

31. Discovering that a wild raccoon is trapped inside your underwear.

32. Dreaming that you have to go to the bathroom really bad and then having your dream end by imagining that you feel great relief.

33. Having your back yard selected as the site for this year's world-wide jamboree for skunks.

34. Having your wife replace your Crunch Berries with sushi for breakfast.

35. Being unable to find a Kleenex or handkerchief after having an explosive, gooey sneeze while being interviewed by Barbara Walters on national TV.

36. Biting into what you thought was a Twinkie and seeing the other half of your daughter's hamster in your hand.

37. Doing a belly flop into an empty swimming pool.

38. Being sold as a slave in some underdeveloped country so your husband can pay for his truck.

39. Being sold as a slave in some far-away land to enable your wife to buy clothes and pay for her spa membership.

40. After delicate brain surgery, being beaned by a 95 M.P.H. fastball.

41. Going outside to enjoy the sunrise for the first time in 700 years and turning to dust the instant the first rays hit your black cape.

42. Chowing down on your dinner at an exclusive, $50.00-a-plate restaurant, and finding the collar of your dog, Max, who came up missing a few weeks earlier, in one of the side dishes.

43. Having your artificial knees, transplanted liver, and pacemaker repossessed because you're delinquent on your medical bills.

44. Exploring a cool cave in South Eastern Nevada and realizing too late that it's a storage facility for nuclear waste.

45. Having your children taken away and placed in a foster home run by rodents or wannabe rock stars.

46. Waking up inside a burning apartment and remembering that you hid all of your money, plus 700 pounds of dynamite, under your bed.

47. Having the time machine you're riding in get stuck in the Jurassic Period.

48. As you climb out of the shower, accidentally knocking down a wasps nest with your towel and then finding that the kids have locked the bathroom door from the outside as a prank.

There. Doesn't that make you feel better?

"Am I Geezing?" You Ask

This is a question that many middle aged people have asked themselves during quiet moments while waxing introspective, or recovering from gall bladder surgery. They feel that they need to know whether or not it's time to get all worked up about being a geezer, or even whether or not they should be reading this book.

The other day, Bill (not his real name) got into his car. And then he got back out of his car to go get his keys. He then got back into his car, and then got back out of his car when he remembered he needed the garage door opener. He then opened the garage door, started his car, and then turned it off again so he could go get his pants on, after which he started it again and drove into town. He then began to try every memory trick he knew to recall the reason why he had come, or if "Town" was the place he should really be. During this moment of deep thought, he pondered, "Could I be geezing?"

The obvious answer is "yes." And you, dear reader could be too. If you worry that you might have crossed the threshold into geezerhood, here are some more case studies which might give you a clue.

Case Study #1: Ruth's friend called to invite her to go to Las Vegas to gamble. They discussed and planned every detail of the trip: prices, hotels, transportation, tours, meals.

Soon after, Ruth's friend went shopping to buy herself some clothes, sent money to the travel agent and did everything else to prepare for this fun vacation.

Meanwhile, Ruth did none of this because she knew that when all was said and done, like always, when it came right down to it, she would just come up with some lame excuse not to go, such as the cat will need to be fed. And besides, it's just too much effort. Ruth is geezing.

Case Study #2: Melvin turns off the TV, brushes his teeth, puts on his jammies, answers a telemarketer on the phone trying to sell him a Medicare supplement, reads from his Geezerhood book by Ben Goode...precisely the same bed time ritual he's performed thousands of times. He then goes to sleep.

Just before midnight, he's awakened by a molecule of falling dust. Since he's now wide awake, he hears the neighbors' dog barking, a few flies buzzing, his wife's dandruff particles clanging loudly onto her pillow, and a gang of white corpuscles rushing to attack a blob of bacteria inside one of the capillaries in his big toe. As he gets up to go to the bathroom for the 7th time, he realizes that he's through getting any actual sleep for the night.

During the next few hours until sunrise, while staring at the ceiling, his mind will cover thousands of trivial things: his failure to grease his fishing reel, which over-the-counter headache medication is best, and whether or not he should feed rat poison to the neighbor's dog. However, he probably won't contemplate the concept of geezing...but he should, because he clearly is...and you could be too.

Case Study #3: Jack is building a shed. He has misplaced his tape measure. So, of course, he calls out: "Chris!" to his daughter who he noticed has just come by to check on him. Chris gently reminds her father, Jack, that she's not Chris. His name is actually "Reggie", and that Chris was in fact, his sister before she died 40 years earlier from a drug overdose.

To this Jack naturally responds, "So he was. It's just that you remind me so much of him."

To which Chris, er...Reggie responds: "Her!"

And so it goes, when you're geezing. ◆

Advantages of Being a Geezer - or - Why You Should be Thrilled to Have Finally Reached the Point Where You Don't Have to Worry About Who's Running in the Next Election

In spite of the fact that aging has some liabilities, in our effort to gain perspective, we must acknowledge that there are also some advantages. The following are just a few that I thought of one day when I was bored:

You can finally get even with your kids for when **you** had to change **their** diapers.

You don't have to make any more house payments. Before they can get through the lengthy process of evicting you, you'll already be dead or they'll just move you into a rest home, which they planned to do anyway.

You are probably past the stage when you'll get acne.

You can insult people any time you want. They'll just write it off as Alzheimer's or crotchitiness.

If they take away your drivers license, you won't have to worry about paying any more insurance premiums.

You can stay out as late as you want and party.

You don't have to worry about your weight, fashion, etc...No matter how much you knock yourself out to look good, no one will care.

You don't ever have to work road construction again.

You can stop brushing your teeth, using deodorant, shaving your legs, etc...If you're disgusting, it's expected.

You don't have to get a bunch of shots for school.

___

You can vote and lobby for every government hand-out known to man. Demand double social security and full medical benefits at no cost, argue for free quarters for slot machines, and a government-financed chauffeur...Remember: you'll be dead soon so you won't be around to hear the next generation whine about having to pay for it all.

___

You can drive recklessly; it's expected.

___

For you, there are no laws. If you want to, you can try all of the fun, illegal stuff you couldn't get away with when you were younger. Feel free to shop lift, poison your neighbor's yapping mutt, wander around naked in public, drive at double the speed limit-in construction zones, go window peeping, and assassinate unwanted politicians. Time has proven that most people dismiss such behavior in old fogies as "senility" or dementia. Even if they don't, since a 5 year sentence is effectively a life sentence to an old geezer, most judges will suspend any really hard time if you promise to be good in the future.

They can't suspend your driver's license if you don't have one.

You can abuse your body and not be expected to feel guilty. Smoking, using heroine, eating yummy, yet unhealthy foods, being promiscuous, and leading a sedentary lifestyle are all okay. Remember: There are probably no degenerative diseases that are fast enough to catch up with you at your age.

You can sleep in...forever if you want to. No one will care.

You know that most things are more trouble than they're worth.

You get to enjoy watching your kids deal with their rebellious teenagers, get no sleep, and juggle finances.

You no longer have to save money. Instead, you can focus on getting it all spent and running up huge debts before you die.

You don't have to go to the dentist any more because you have no teeth. If you do still have some teeth left, you can pull them. ◆

4 Using Your Years of Marriage Experience to Make Your Spouse Happy

I don't know.

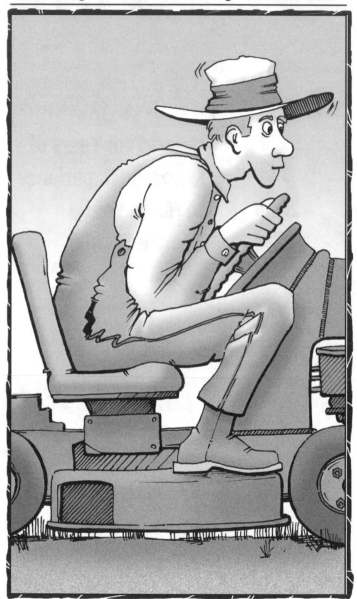

5 Although there are Worse Things than Being Older than Dirt, it Still Stinks to Have Aches and Pains

All of my life I've enjoyed gardening. However, as I have aged, I have had to enjoy it with gradually increasing physical limitations. For example, I have to do my lifting carefully, using my legs to reduce the strain on my bad back. I bought a self-propelled lawn mower to compensate for my reduced strength and stamina. I no longer pull stickery weeds because they hurt my fingers and because I always hated pulling them anyway. I no longer climb fruit trees because of my vertigo and because I black out occasionally from low blood sugar and fall. (Besides, such falls tend to break perfectly good pear-producing limbs on the way down and shatter formerly useful bones.) I wear a helmet and shoulder pads when I drive so the automatic shoulder harness doesn't beat me unconscious when it slides over my head as I close the door. I no longer open pesticide lids with my teeth because the chemicals are hard on my ulcer and because my teeth  come out. And, of course, I'm careful not to take the lid of the septic tank off because it smells so bad.

Being forced by increasing physical limitations to make these changes has caused me to reflect on growing older and the relative advantages and disadvantages of living to a ripe old age. On the one hand, ever since being symbolically hurled aside onto the trash heap of life like so much used garbage, I have had much more free time to pursue activities that I've always wanted to do like gardening, marathon running, demolition derby, surfing, mountain climbing, big-game hunting, bunji-jumping, and pulling malicious pranks on my

neighbors. On the other hand, there's no way I will
have the energy to do these things, I have no
money, and I'll probably die soon. On the one
hand, I have the companionship of my sweet wife
with whom to do fun things. On the other hand, my
lifelong companion is usually sleeping, is never
interested, and repeatedly reminds me that fun
things take way too much effort.

In spite of the fact that I rarely do anything
meaningful, I am still able to enjoy life. If you, too
are the type of person who would like to learn how
to enjoy life with your aches and pains while
growing older, since you obviously don't feel like
doing anything or you probably wouldn't be
reading this book, perhaps I could share with you
an experience I had while gardening the other day.

The Experience And Wisdom
of an Old Guy

Not long ago I went outside to poison the
gophers and on my way, I noticed that I had
forgotten to turn off the water the night before. As
a result, it had completely flooded my strawberries
and the neighbor's basement. On my way over to
turn off the spicket, I accidentally stepped on a
worm hole, which caused me to lose my balance

and fall backwards, flopping flat on my back onto a bed of biting ants.

Many gardeners would have picked themselves up cussing their clumsiness and bad luck, but not me. I lied there gazing up into the beautiful, brown sky, actually savoring this rare moment by imagining what interesting and artistic shapes the clouds would be making if I could only see them up above the smog. As I was reveling in this precious moment of life, I must have dosed off because some time later I was awakened with a start due to a feeling of wetness. My first thought was that I had better sneak into the house to change my pants before someone saw and accused me of being incontinent. But then I remembered the spicket which I had planned to turn off and sat up in a panic only to realize that my wetness didn't come from either of these causes. Actually, my wife's wretched mutt, Poopsie, who just turned 91 in doggie years and who doesn't see or smell so well, had apparently mistaken me for an inanimate object and peed in my ear.

The profound meaning I gleaned from this experience is that you shouldn't get too obsessed about things like your gardening; it takes too much effort. Besides when you become this pathetic, all of the little mutts in your life will probably just symbolically pee in your ear anyway... and getting older and having innumerable aches and pains really stinks. ◆

Bad Ideas For Old Geezers

All around us we see examples of remarkable things being done by old geezers: a 90 year old grandma finally graduating from high school, an 88-year-old great great grandpa of 72 completing his first 10-K run, a 79-year-old grandpa getting caught shoplifting, my cousin, Blanche, getting completely up from her chair and onto her feet unassisted.

While it certainly warms our hearts to know that there are still a few amusing things old people can do, we feel it's important to warn our readers about some of the things they probably shouldn't try once they lose their faculties. Here are just a few things we don't think you should do any more now that you're as old as dirt-or if you're still doing them, you should probably stop.

Bad Ideas for Geezers:

1. Holding on to car bumpers and cruising behind on your skate board.

2. Smashing beer cans against your head.

3. In order to add some variety to your life, taking your customary long afternoon nap on a slab down at the morgue.

4. Using a hot iron to straighten out the wrinkles on your husband's face.

5. Saving the food that has been stuck on your dentures for later.

6. Sneaking a toke on a hashish pipe by inhaling it through your oxygen tank.

7. Whacking a wasps nest with your cane.

8. Undergoing breast enhancement surgery...unless you can convince the doctors to use implants filled with helium.

9. Using a 220 outlet as the power source for your pace maker.

10. Wiring your hearing aid to a teenager's stereo.

11. Driving your neighbor's motor home into the lake so you can go fishing from the roof.

12. In order to double the life of your Depends® and save a bunch of money, turning them inside out and wearing them a second time.

13. Taking out your false teeth and using them to clip your toe nails in public.

14. Wearing a Speedo®.

15. Wearing a bikini.

16. Rolling over a land mine in your wheel chair.

17. Getting into a feud with your neighbor, "Igor," a professional wrestler, over the fact his sprinklers are leaving water spots on the tires of your "68 Buick Riviera.

18. Going to the mortuary to try to pick up girls.

19. Going downtown wearing a Raiders' jacket and painting gang symbols on your bald head.

20. Eating 10 pounds of cheese in one sitting.

21. Using your mouth to crack Brazil nuts when you have no teeth.

22. Adding two-four-barrel carburetors and then filling the gas tank of your '68 Pontiac Bonneville with nitro.

> **23. Dragging Main Street looking for trouble**

> **24. Getting into a feud with your neighbor, "Jack," the IRS agent, over the fact that his kids left their roller skates on your lawn and threatening to get even with him.**

> **25. Staying up all night partying.**

> **26. Using battery acid to get the stains off your dentures.**

> **27. Shooting a 30/06 off in a bank vault.**

> **28. Volunteering for duty as a speed bump at the local elementary school.**

> **29. Hang gliding without a helmet.**

30. While pastel pink or blue hair is O.K., having yours done in green, yellow or purple...and in a Mowhawk is a bad idea.

31. Body surfing a volcano.

32. Buying your blood pressure medication from the local cocaine dealer down on the street.

33. Attempting a Guinness world record for streaking across Antarctica.

34. Seeing how many of your buddies you can squeeze into a phone booth.

35. Burying the needle in your Winnebago to see what it can do.

36. Driving with an attitude and flipping everyone else off.

37. Driving at all.

38. Surfing the Internet in search of a corn massage.

I Remember When

The following are a few reminiscences or hallucinations sent to us by some of our faithful readers:

George A. Custard VII from Waterloo, Iowa writes, "I remember during the War, there were no car tires so we had to drive on pork and bean-can lids or sliced salami. Once, when we were cruising out across the plains, we had a blow out. A bunch of Indians swooped down just a whooping and hollering. It turned out that they were just hungry and their self-esteem was low, so we shared our salami tires with them and they gave us a ride home on their buffalo."

Frankie Roosevelt XII from Grape-Wrath, California says: "In the old days, we used to work 25 or 26 hours a day digging ditch. I never did figure out what the boss man wanted with all those ditches, but since it was during the depression we were happy to have the work...and frankly real proud of our blisters."

Betty Dyes from Leavenworth, Kansas writes: "I remember when we were younger, we used to love to go around to all the houses in the neighborhood and do "mischief" as we called it. This usually consisted of a few harmless little childhood pranks like putting sugar into neighbor's gas tanks or pounding a few spikes into neighbors' tires. Then we would sneak around and put a little broken glass into the neighbors' dog and cat food, and then mix a little motor oil with arsenic and poison the town's water supply. And then sometimes we would break a few store windows and lay some bear traps around the elementary school play ground while we were walking home."

Wilma Flintstone from Bedrock, New Mexico remembered what it was like the day the dinosaurs died: "I cried all day," she said. "But, in the end it probably turned out for the best. The world would have eventually run out of whale oil and soon had nothing to use to power our cars except for Fred."

Robert Cratchet from Rat's Flank, Mississippi reminisced: "When I was a boy, we were so poor that all my parents could afford to get me for a pet was a worm. I named him Willard. I loved that worm! He was the only friend I had. Then I saw in a Life Magazine how some kids painted cool things on the shells of their pet turtles. Being young and inexperienced and not knowing any better, I decided to paint "Willard" on the back of my worm. I doubt he even survived the half hour under the power sander, let alone being dipped into gray auto primer."

Betty Rubble from Bedrock, Arkansas reminisced: "I remember being so poor that the only house we could afford was a cave in the rocks. In fact, the only cave available when we got turned out of our gravel pit, already had a saber-toothed tiger living in it. We lured it out one night using one of our neighbors, who we didn't like, as bait. Then we hurried and shoved a rock over the entrance. That cat whined all night."

Wayne Johns of Neck d' Rouge, Idaho remembers: "Back in the early 40's, the war effort took away all of the toothpaste. The soldiers needed it to shave with, for caulking holes in their tents, and of course, to stick stamps to their letters since there was no glue. So we had to make do with things like Mr. Clean and an occasional squashed stink bug's thorax to brush our teeth. And, of course we had to share our tooth brushes with all of the barn yard animals."

Isaac Abramson from Alexandria, Virginia recalled: "My Grandpa Moses used to like to sit around and tell us kids stories about the good old days when he was a lad. They were always playing tricks on Pharaoh...like the time they turned all the frogs loose and then dropped a snake in the throne room."

W. Ginsburg from Washington D.C. writes: "As a young boy I always dreamed of becoming a great lawyer when I grew up, like my father. Unfortunately, Dad was unable to provide economic assistance because he was pulling a life sentence for fraud. But I never gave up on my dream. Unfortunately, while working in a child slave labor camp to save money for law school, I was involved in an industrial accident in which my head was smashed and my brain was severely damaged. Since that time, I have been living the life of a garden vegetable, having been kept alive solely because nobody has the guts to pull the plug on the machines at the hospital. Since it was worthless to me, I let the medical students remove my brain so they could use it to practice rugby. (You have probably guessed by now that I am having my mom write this letter.)

But back to my story...To my surprise, because of my extraordinary level of diversity, Yale University's aptitude profiler identified me as a perfect scholarship prospect for their law school. Thanks to them, I was able to realize my dream of pursuing a career in law. I am currently a well-respected member of the faculty at Yale and a regular guest on Geraldo."

L.H. Harry Lee MMXXVII of Buzzard Itch, Virginia remembers: "When I was a boy one summer, we were all getting ready to fight Quantrill's Raiders when an epidemic of the plague went through the area. It wiped out 90% of the citizens in the county and my pet hog, Bruce. It also killed all the enemy soldiers. I'll never forget how disappointed we were about having to stay home and pluck chickens."

James Carvilleski, of Rancid Creek, Arkansas writes: "When I was a young man, we had problems with varmints getting into our chickens. Me and my brother, Floyd, decided to sleep in the coop and try to catch them. After a couple of weeks of sleeping out there, we decided that it wasn't really so bad-other than having mom make us scrape the chicken droppings off our faces before we could go to school. Besides, the food was pretty good. So we stayed all summer.

Call me old fashioned if you want, but from time to time, I still like to sleep out under the open chickens."

James also writes: "We also had problems with mice and birds getting together and beating up my mom's poodle, Fifi. Since we had done so well defending the chickens, me and my brother, Floyd, got elected to sleep outside and protect the guard-dog. At first, we didn't like it at all, but after a while, we decided it wasn't so bad. Call me old fashioned if you want, but even though I'm married, I still spend many nights sleeping out in the old dog house."

James Carvilleski Jr. from Rancid Creek, Arkansas, reminisces: "When I was a boy, my brother, Floyd and I had the hots for these two sisters, Edith and Beulah. I can't begin to tell you how excited we were when they finally let us get close enough to wash their cars...and mow their lawns...and do their laundry...and wash their dishes...and clean their corrals...and slop their hogs...and do their home work. But then, one day they got married and their husbands beat us up, so now we sleep outside in the bushes.

He also remembers: "Once, when some new neighbors came by to visit, Dad and Mom had me and my brother, Floyd, hide in the old fridge out back. (Although they didn't tell us, I think they wanted us to jump out and surprise them or something.) The problem was, when we tried to make our grand entry, the door wouldn't open. We survived for two weeks on mildew, night crawlers, and a couple of Tupperware bowls of 3-year-old potato salad, which actually wasn't so bad. Bless her heart, Mom finally remembered us. Dad was pretty mad. Mostly at himself, I think. ◆

How To Impress Young People

Many older people, especially aging baby boomers, feel a desperate compulsion to do everything in their power to impress younger people. Over the past few years, we have studied this phenomenon, and from all of the literature, we have gleaned some successful ways this can be done. If you feel compelled, here are the tried and proven ways for old people to wow young people:

1. Be Rich.

2. Be hip.

3. Dress well.

4. By diligently working out; develop your abdominal muscles into a "six pak."

5. Like really over-use words like "like."

6. Know your hip music; better yet, learn to like terrible music. Wear headphones and turn them way up while you listen to bands with names like "Bleeding Gums" or "Puke and the Mucous Spickets."

7. Live on the edge. Show your contempt for danger by going into establishments which have a "Microwave Oven In Use" sign on the door.

8. Drive way too fast and have an attitude.

9. Wear Spandex biker shorts and look good in them.

10. Become a psychic. It's easy. Just tell every woman who calls that her boyfriend is cheating on her. Odds are he is and even if he's not, let him try to prove that one.

11. Be in a constant state of rebellion against the establishment. Wear T-shirts with slogans like, "Age Against the Machine," or "No Fair!"

12. Ride your skateboard or your Harley to BINGO.

13. Really get into pro wrestling...better yet, become a pro wrestler yourself. This could be an important first step toward a rewarding career in politics.

14. Be good at video games. Waste thousands of hours trying to get to the next level or trying to kill the blob before he splits up and takes away three of your lives.

15. Be young. ◆

Reasons to Feel Optimistic About the World's Future While in the Hands of the Rising Generation... After You're Dead

Sorry, we can't think of any right now.

10

It Stinks to Have to Eat Rotten Food

I went to my daughter's place the other night for dinner. Out of respect for my borderline diabetes, high blood pressure, clogged and hardened arteries, poor circulation, indigestion, and chronic heartburn, she fixed white stuff, light-yellow stuff, and bland, green stuff, all of which tasted pretty good- kinda like a filet of tofu seasoned with Tums on open faced cardboard.

The sad thing is, my daughter is actually a pretty good cook; at least she used to be. She's perfectly capable of preparing a good roast, mashed potatoes and gravy, and a cherry pie.

Out of love and respect, I ate the stuff she fixed. Then after poking some asparagus spears up my nose and getting out my rubber chicken to lighten things up, I began a fatherly discussion about the fact that dying suddenly of a stroke doesn't sound so bad when compared with living to be 106 and having to eat shoe box lids. Of course, this started an even more rousing discussion bordering on an argument, where it became apparent that my kids suspect that it's about time for me to turn over my bank accounts and be dragged kicking and screaming to  the Shady Bunion nursing home. But listen. The only point I was trying to make was that it really stinks to have to spend your last few years, which might wind up being wretched anyway, eating bad food.

Having spent hundreds of boring hours worrying about how to pretend to eat healthy food which tastes lousy, while, in reality, sneaking good, unhealthy food while no one is looking, and since I speak occasionally to some of my few living friends about this, I have determined that many of them have the same attitude. So I decided that it was time to unleash good old American ingenuity on this problem of bad food and come up with a real high tech solution.

My Solution

My proposed solution can best be illustrated with a personal experience. The other day when I was tending myself and no one was looking, I went to this place that makes great pizza. They're a little bit expensive, but that's okay because they use twice as much cheese as any one else. Then, they load that baby down with pepperoni, sausage, Canadian bacon and every other kind of fatty, red meat known to man, throw on a few peppers, onions and olives, sprinkle it with just the perfect amount of spices, and then cook it to perfection. When I eat there, I can barely wait to pick up a large piece because the cheese is so melted that I have to use two hands to keep it from looping down my arm. This makes the mozzarella strings stretch from the pan clear to my mouth.

I am beginning to drool just thinking about my last meal there, where I chomped down on all that cheese and other stuff and chewed it and savored that wonderful taste and texture...And then, a split second after I got it into my mouth, I realized that it had just come out of a 2000 degree oven and that it was too late to do anything about the fact that I had fried all the membranes from my teeth to my tonsils, maybe even charred them black.

In spite of the fact that this pizza was the most yummy thing I had eaten recently, and that it was too pricey to waste, I wanted to yell and scream and spit it out, but there were way too many people around me. So I tried to gracefully spit it into a napkin so that no one could see. However, the slobber and oil and a pepperoni all stuck to my chin, except for the part which slid into my lap. But the point is, I know that for this evening and for the next few days, pizza and everything else I eat will pretty much taste the same. I have cooked my taste buds to numbness. "Will they ever fully recover?" I wonder. Even after having repeated this process many times, I'm still not sure.

Over the years, I bet if me and my geezing buddies were to chow down on pizza for say, three meals a day, we would probably burn our taste buds like this a few hundred more times. Therefore, I believe it's possible that old people like myself could actually get to the point where we could have no healthy, functioning taste buds remaining. Thus, they could feed us that bland, healthy stuff and we wouldn't even know the difference. I say it's worth a try. ◆

Fun Things to do While You're Waiting to Die Which Don't Require too Much Effort

Get with some of your buddies and start a wheezing quartet.

See if you can remember how to tap out the Declaration of Independence in Morse code using your cane.

Create TV art by holding the channel changer button down with your thumb and watching the pictures flash buy.

Tie a nostalgic camp-quilt using the obituaries of your former friends which you've cut out of the newspapers as material.

Poke bubble gum up your nose and see how big you can make your bubbles.

Study the mating habits of geraniums or pompous grass.

Watch your grandkids play computer games.

See how many creative ways you can come up with to clog your toilet. Then count how many different people the landlord sends over to try to unclog them.

Check to see if you can still fog a mirror and then, assuming you can, write a novel in the mist.

Float face down in your swimming pool and set your stopwatch to see how long it takes paramedics to respond.

Stack rocks.

Eat great tasting, yet terribly unhealthy food.

Take your time enjoying a good bowel movement-up to 4-years if you want.

Spend a few days trying to clear out your sinuses by using your well-developed, veteran snorting skills.

Write a biography revealing the private lives of the county maintenance workers.

Try to slowly drink yourself to death on Gatorade or, if you're lactose intolerant, whole milk.

Reorganize all of the food in your refrigerator.

Make a list of 1000 worthy charities and poor people; and then give them a brief, once-in-a-lifetime thrill which, unfortunately will probably last just a day or two, by sending each of them a check for ten million dollars on an account that you have already closed.

Build a world-class cockroach collection.

See how many different and interesting shapes you can create using your cat's tail.

Call every psychic hot line in America and pretend you're someone different while talking to each one. If you're still bored, when you finish listening to their baloney, you can talk to them for hours telling them interesting stories from the good old days.

Before the animal rights groups get all their money, initiate a class-action lawsuit against all leather shoe manufacturers because of the emotional trauma you've suffered over the years because of corns and blisters.

Put large, dragon tattoos on all of your friends.

Start your own charity. Choose a worthy cause such as "Rat and Roach Rights," Protecting the Methane Layer, or Equal Rights for Whiners.

Try to invent a device that will play a 33 1/3 RPM record on your CD player.

Train for some esoteric Olympic event being introduced to the games in the near future. Get in shape for events like: Rhythmic Bowling, Downhill Keyboarding, Australian Rules Cake Decorating, Greco/Roman Super Mario, or Synchronized Roller Derby.

Build your own oxygen-tank apparatus from stuff you have lying around the garage.

Invest the time needed to do research to develop a new kind of medication by randomly mixing different quantities of your old pills and medications and testing them on all the extra politicians and bureaucrats.

Try to biologically mutate in some important way.

Go fishing for salmon in your bathtub or irrigation ditch.

Before your mind is completely gone, do the research necessary to find a cure for hiccups, broken hearts, absent-mindedness, cancer, procrastination, or some other debilitating disease.

Polish up your skills on the accordion.

It Stinks
to be Broke

There are two kinds of older people in this world: eccentric rich people...and old coots. Being an old coot with no money can be tough because so very few people ever take you seriously. You probably have to do your own laundry, cut your own hair, do your own exercises, remove your own tonsils, drive your own car and even take your own medication. This is not fair. Because we want to get in on the ground-level of this movement to make everything in the world fair, we have come up with a ground-breaking idea.

We believe that this is a great solution because first, there are many, many younger people who are planning to go on in life and make a career out of getting older. What better training could they have than spending a couple of years doing odd jobs for people who already have years of experience at it, much like a political intern in Washington DC would do learning the art of talking out of both sides of his mouth.

I know that many of you are not wealthy. You fear that you don't have enough money to afford your own intern. Before you panic, we want to remind you that politicians don't pay for theirs. Remember; interns are working for free so that they can get good connections. Therefore, if you want a free old-person-training intern, you just have to be well-connected.

The only problem with this idea arises when the old person is well connected, but unfortunately, only to broke old geezers like himself. If this sounds like you, you may have to pay for your intern after all. Never fear, however. I have a fund raising idea for all the old codgers who are currently struggling to pay the dental floss bill:

A Fund Raising Idea

Sell technology to the Chinese. It looks to me like you can make billions of dollars doing this. I know that the reason why so many people don't solve their financial problems this way is probably because they feel that they don't have any valuable technology to sell. I say it doesn't matter. All you have to do is make some up. They'll never know it's bogus. They speak Chinese.

Just to get you thinking, here are a few of my ideas: (Before you start, however, you may want to file to run for President or Congress in order to make it appear to the Chinese that your technology could have some strategic military value.) Next, pick an essential, life-or-death piece of technology like, say...Beanie Babies. Develop a phony blue print explaining how to make them. Then explain to the Chinese that with your blue prints and their billions of starving people who are willing to work for a bowl of rice, they can mass-produce them by the millions, flood the Beanie Baby market and quickly wipe us out by ruining our economy. Then find some Buddhist monks to do your marketing.

There is really no way to get hurt on this because if you should get yourself into a little trouble, you can always start a legal defense account by holding fund raising dinners in Hollywood using current celebrities and old ones from Hollywood Squares. As a side benefit, you will probably get to meet Barbara Streisand and Tom Hanks.

Regardless, whether or not you ever get to the point that you can afford an intern, we all have to admit' it stinks to be broke. Many people who are broke don't like it at all. ◆

13 How to Make Your Relationship With Your Spouse Come Alive During Your Golden Years

Sorry, I don't know.

The Scandal of the Millennium

Last year in America, more than 20,000 people drowned. Another 15,000 died from pneumonia, and nearly 70,000 more were killed in bunji chord accidents or by bad jokes. A whole bunch more, millions I'm told, were killed by the air bags in their cars and from smelling peanut fumes while in airliners. As shocking and inaccurate as these statistics are, they pale in comparison to the greatest scandal our country has ever known. We get all worked up when a few thousand Americans die from cigarette smoking, suicide, or perfume fumes or after committing suicide from smoking perfume fumes. Why, oh, why, then, aren't millions and billions of dollars being spent on research to stop the leading killer in America today?

"What is this decimating scourge?" You ask. Is it Aids, hate crimes, gout, or failure to post signs on restaurant doors warning that microwave ovens are in use? No, it is a disease that's right before your eyes only you just can't see it without your bifocals: It's OLD AGE and I'll wager hardly a family alive has not lost at least one precious loved one to this ruthless and debilitating scourge.

"So, why isn't the president doing anything about this?" You ask. "Why doesn't he feel our pain?" It gives me an cerebral hemorrhoid just thinking about it. I've worried and worried about this until it occurred to me that the only reason why something this entertaining, with this much political capital was not being blasted at us nightly in the media is that there must be some kind of cover up or scandal...or else it's none of our business. That being the case, I decided that the only reasonable thing for me to do was to use my vast journalistic resources to look into this problem and see why it was that all of the deaths, carnage, and geezercides are being symbolically swept under the rug like so many dead cockroaches.

To start with, I decided to begin looking where the trail wouldn't already be cold. I tried to interview one of the people with first -hand knowledge of the suffering and misery: the most recent victims of the disease. To my horror, I couldn't find even one victim who had died of old age who wasn't already dead and therefore refusing to comment. So I had no choice but to do what all other modern journalists, who don't want to make any effort do: I interviewed a defense lawyer.

The problem with this approach was that this guy proceeded to use big words that I couldn't understand or spell. But, I kind of got the impression that he was mad because law enforcement people and the religious right are racist scum and because other people have no right to judge his clients who have only committed mass murders, acts of terrorism, thefts, treason, bestiality, perjury, obstruction of justice, and driving under the influence because we have all at one time or another in our lives been guilty of lusting in our hearts or eating red meat. And besides, prosecutors, judges, soccer moms, faithful husbands and wives, Kenneth Starr, and conservative radio talk show hosts, should all be disenfranchised for not being ethnically diverse and for not allowing librarians to show pornography or violent video games to kids, or for refusing to allow doctors to help kill sick people.

I left the interview feeling suspiciously uneasy about why he had been so willing to talk. "Why was it he didn't feel threatened with death or the appointment of a special prosecutor?" I wondered. I also noticed right away that either he wasn't interested or else he didn't know anything about any mammoth cover up, or that if he did, he was keeping mum. It soon became apparent to me that I needed to conjure up some other source for my information or else choose another topic.

As I walked home, discouraged in the pouring rain, it began to dawn on me that the water was running down my back clear into my underwear and that maybe I didn't need to pay the big bucks and run all over town looking for an expert after all. It suddenly occurred to me that everything anyone wants to know about this and anything else in the world was right in front of me all along, right there under my fingers where every adult in America, provided that he has access to a helpful child or adolescent, could readily access every bit of information on any academic subject- along with some great Playboy bunnies, voyeuristic insights, Kama Sutra, S&M, preventing unwanted pregnancies, creating unwanted pregnancies, 1000 perverse fetishes complete with excellent graphics, and all the kids' grades from school: ON THE INTERNET!

Fearing that I would forget about this great idea, I hobbled over and got my 11 year old grandson out of school to help me. Thanks to his expertise, after only a few stops to retrieve information about building a Hydrogen bomb in the basement, converting a BB gun into an automatic rifle, and making a delivery system for chemical and biological weapons, and after hacking into the C.I.A.'s main data banks just to show how easy it was, to my delight, he was able to get directly into a White House chat room! (Come to find out, the kids in my grandson's 6th grade class have been regular visitors to this chat room for years.) To my further surprise, at that moment the Clintons and their operatives were all there hanging out in this very cyber spot! What luck!

After a quick message or two to catch up on the latest from Brandi, who is pregnant, and Jackie, who wants to break up with Matt, we were able to focus in on the most powerful leaders of the free world. At the time, they were sitting around using White House phones to call past financial donors with deep pockets to invite them to bring their money bags to some cool fund raisers which couldn't be called fund raisers, and to call focus groups to get public opinion to help make important foreign policy decisions, and to call the joint chiefs of staff to begin another round of bombing in some heretofore unknown third-world country in order to head off another possible decline in presidential popularity and divert public attention away from the latest oval office scandal...when the phone rang.

Amid the noise from giggling interns and Larry Flint, who was meeting with Yassar Arafat planning strategy for exposing hypocrisy in the Republican party, a voice came over the speaker phone. This was a voice familiar to all of us, which every American has come to know and love; it was the voice of a major long distance telemarketer trying to persuade The President of the United

States to change long distance companies. Tears of pride welled up in my eyes as I witnessed this moment of decisive leadership as our president, after conducting a quick opinion poll and with the results firmly in hand, invited the telemarketer to bring his boss to next week's Democratic fund raiser.

Tragically, after he hung up, it became clear that in addition to trivial errors in judgment like selling military secrets to China, non-medicinal use of marijuana, and some major league philandering, our president was also involved in serious criminal activity. He was at the vortex of the world-wide cover up of the deaths of millions of old people.

To summarize the facts of the case: the government now has hard data proving beyond a reasonable doubt that perjury, obstruction of justice, and the use of government officials and perverted publishers to try to intimidate potential damaging witnesses do not rise to the level of impeachment and that because of a high-profile celebrity ad campaign, combined with a healthy dose of feigned presidential compassion, all the youth in America will soon quit drugs and smoking, and start turning in their math assignments.

"Well and good," you say, but these insidious statistics reveal another problem even worse than the 12,000 adolescents dying annually from drive-by shootings: namely that if people stop smoking, fewer will die young, which means that sooner or later more of them will begin drawing out their social security which means that the baby boomers will never get to draw out any benefits because the money will be gone.

For the first time in his administration, the president of the United States was painted into a box. He was staring the hard reality in the face that it wasn't possible to eliminate all of the causes of death in America today AND keep social security fully funded. Something would have to give. Since the old people had already survived the Great Depression, sacrificed so much to win World War II, and lived through another new season of network TV, he naturally figured that they probably wouldn't mind cowboying up one more time to take care of the problem of old people living too long.

Naturally, the president had no choice but to have the attorney general claim executive privilege to suppress the data which proves that he sold military secrets to Tahiti in order to finance his daughter's trip to Europe, because it contained personally embarrassing information damaging to national security, which showed the number of people dying in America from old age. Now it all made sense to me. And hopefully it will to you too because I don't have any more space for this. ◆

 More Perspective... Some Reasons Why You Should Be Happy Even if You're Dead

You are most likely not hanging tied to a fraying rope over a vat of boiling oil.

You are probably not being eaten by mink.

You probably didn't make your doctor really mad, so he didn't remove your brain or sew your kidneys to your forehead.

There are many people on the planet who have never met you, and, therefore, can't possibly know what a big jerk you are.

79

You are not being forced to eat worm poop.

You most likely didn't drink a quart of paint thinner, thinking it was club soda, last night.

Your mom probably still likes you and hasn't completely given up on you.

If she has, she probably isn't trying to poison you.

If she is, apparently she hasn't succeeded yet.

You are not the former Jimmy Hoffa.

Unless you are Evander Holyfield, a part of your ear isn't being digested by Mike Tyson.

Right now, you are most likely not tied to the railroad tracks.

You haven't been pushed off of the
World Trade Center recently.

If you live on the street, you represent a
fairly large voting block.

Jumping Pihrana probably don't live
in your toilet.

Roaches don't weigh 500 pounds.

You most likely didn't just wake up on the beach
with no memory of the past.

At times you are capable of
rational thought.

Your spouse is probably not an insect.

Our President is not a duck... I don't think.

Questions and Answers

Q. I woke up this morning and reached for my shoe on the floor near my bed because that's where I keep my false teeth at night. Not only were my teeth missing, but so were my shoes. What could have happened? What should I do? If I don't find them soon, I could be late for BINGO or miss it all together.

A. For starters, don't panic. You are just experiencing something that routinely happens to all senior citizens. You probably just died in the night and don't know it. Either that or else the tooth fairy got confused and took your shoes along with your teeth when she flew by on her rounds in the middle of the night.

If you should happen to find out later today that you are still alive, when you go to BINGO, if you look closely, you will notice that many of your associates might also be dead. Since most dead people have no use for their BINGO tokens, take theirs, put them into your mouth and rattle them around like gizzard stones to grind your food. You can use this dinosaur method of chewing until you find your teeth. Don't worry. If the tooth fairy has them, she'll probably realize her mistake and return them in a couple of days.

Q. Yesterday as I brought a prune up to my mouth to take a bite, I was shocked and depressed to realize that the prune actually had fewer wrinkles than my face. What's more, my husband says it may now even be better looking. Is there anything I can do to get rid of these unsightly wrinkles...or, if that's not possible, to take these uppity prunes down a few notches by making them look worse?

A. Years ago there would have been nothing you could have done about your wrinkly problem. Fortunately, you have been blessed to live during a time of high technology; you have many options. For starters, I have seen some epidermically disadvantaged older folk chew with their mouths open and then swallow their prunes, pit and all, out of contempt. But if you want to do something truly vindictive to make them look exceptionally bad, soak the prune in rancid pond water and then show it to your husband magnified thousands of times under a microscope. This will make him glad that your face doesn't also have scary looking microscopic creatures crawling all over it. Just don't let him put YOU under the microscope.

Q. When humans get old, they get frail, senile, bald and wrinkly. When dogs get old, they get fat, shaky, gray, and blind. Over the years, I have noticed that you rarely see an old-looking duck. Why do you suppose that is?

A. Since you're obviously so astute, you've undoubtedly also noticed that you've never seen a hairy duck, a toothless duck, a duck with Alzheimer's, a duck that dresses poorly, a duck with a dirty face, or a duck that bowls over 150. You may also have noticed that you rarely see an old-looking pile of dirt, planet, chocolate chip, or glass of water. Keep asking questions like this and before you know it your kids will have you locked away in a rest home and be having a wild time with your money.

Q. Recently, my husband has begun to sleep in until very late in the mornings. When I say late, I mean that he fell asleep last Spring and hasn't been awake since. I think he needs a shower. Do you have any ideas?

A. Relax. This is no big deal. Sleeping disorders are common in older people. Throw a couple of shovels of dirt on him; if that doesn't wake him up, just take it as a sign and keep shoveling.

Q. During our working lives, my husband and I have managed to accumulate a few million dollars which we are planning to donate to the Corporation for Public Broadcasting when we die. But our married kids and their spouses have been acting weird lately since my husband and I have been treated and released from the hospital because of our 5th bout with arsenic poisoning which all probably happened when we ate dinner at our children's house. And then last month we pulled out of the driveway in our car only to discover as we drove down the road that we had no brakes and were it not for the fact that the 500 foot cliff we drove off had an ocean at the bottom, and even though the doors were locked from the outside and reinforced with bunji chords, and even though we had the presence of mind to break a window and swim to safety, later this week came the straw that broke the camel's back. Just before the Ninja guy with the black hood burst into our bedroom trying to kill us with his swords (Fortunately, my husband was able to disarm him with the hand-grenade he always keeps by his bed.), we got a series of threatening letters warning us to include our children in our will. Blanch says our kids are trying to send us a message. I say they're just acting out. What do you say? R. J. Ewing, Dallas, TX.

A. Probably it's just a phase. Kids will do this sort of thing from time to time. For the next few years, just be sure and have a rat, gerbil, lawyer, or telemarketer taste your food before you eat it. ◆

The Ultimate Test of your Geezerhood

1. Which do you find more attractive:
A. Demi Moore in a swimsuit
B. Doris Day in a swimsuit
C. Joan of Ark in a swimsuit
D. Can't remember

2. Which is your favorite beverage:
A. Bavarian Beer
B. Warm Milk
C. Alka Seltzer
D. Can't remember

3. Which describes your biggest worries in life:

A. Thinking of new and exciting things to do on the weekend

B. Being able to afford more of everything than your peers

C. Personal problems at work, paying your bills, possible reasons behind your painful urination, why you don't sleep well, what's causing your short-term memory loss, blacking out, dizziness, impotence, how to function at work through a few more years with severe chronic back pain, not being able to remember your last regular bowel movement, will you have enough money to retire, and the next presidential election

    D. Can't remember

4. Your idea of a fun time is:

    A. New adventures in exotic places with fascinating people

    B. Golf, a brisk walk, or a comfortable rocking chair and a good book

    C. A successful bowel movement

    D. Can't remember

What it means:

    If you scored mostly A's: You are still so young you have no right to complain about anything

    If you scored mostly B's: You have only experienced a small inkling. You can complain if you want to, but only to the very young

    If you scored mostly C's: You are still living, but barely. Complain all you want

    If you scored mostly D's: Thank the nurse who wrote your answers for you. Yes, you just took a test. Wasn't it nice?

Additional Apricot Press Books

'The Truth About Life' Humor Books